National Learning Association
Everything You
Should Know About:
IRELAND AND SCOTLAND
Faster Learning Facts
By: Anne Richards

INTRODUCTION – TELL ME A LITTLE BIT ABOUT IRELAND

Ireland is Europe's second largest island, just after Great Britain, and is also the westernmost country in continental Europe. Ireland's land is split 80/20 into the Republic of Ireland and the United Kingdom, respectively. The northernmost portion of the country is still part of the United Kingdom. Ireland is called

Éire in Irish and the country's official name is the
Republic of Ireland.

WHAT IS THE CAPITAL OF IRELAND?

Dublin is Ireland's capital city. Dublin is famous for its easygoing culture and rich heritage. Many famous authors, native to Dublin, wrote about their hometown over the years: James Joyce, Jonathan Swift and Oscar Wilde to name a few. The city is divided into a north and south side by the River Liffey, which is located in the city's center. The south side population is typically upper class while the north side residents are mostly working class.

WHO WERE THE VIKINGS?

The Vikings were a group of violent, Scandinavian people who raided lands across the globe by sea. The name "Viking" even means a "pirate raid." The Vikings who raided Ireland stole many of the country's treasures including Fanvaig's Casket, which was returned to Ireland years later and now resides in the National Museum of Ireland. Vikings arrived in Ireland around 795 A.D. and ruled there for many years. Vikings even married the Irish, and their bloodline became known as the Irish-Norse people.

WHAT IS IRELAND'S LANDSCAPE LIKE?

When most people think of Ireland they think of lush green fields and wide expanses of rolling hills. In fact, the country is even nicknamed the Emerald Isle because of its green countryside. Since glaciers once covered the country – about 15,000 years ago – towards the western coast of Ireland you'll find damp peat bogs and even the soggy remains of ancient dried up lakes. These wetlands contribute to the lush green nature of Ireland. The country also boasts beautiful, rocky coastlines and majestic mountains.

WHAT TYPE OF GOVERNMENT DOES IRELAND HAVE?

Ireland is a parliamentary democracy. This means that Ireland is a democracy that consists of an elected parliament with a president, or prime minister, at the head of the state. The Parliament makes the laws and the prime minster enforces them. Eighty percent of Ireland is free and governs itself while the northernmost part of the country is governed under United Kingdom rule. The part of the island under the United Kingdom you may still vote in some elections.

WHAT IS AGRICULTURE LIKE IN IRELAND?

Traditionally Ireland was primarily a farming country and although it is not a primary livelihood today, it is still very important to the Irish people. Since the 1950s though, the country has made successful efforts to attract business, making Ireland the second wealthiest nation in the world today! People still farm, mostly barley, which is used for malting, seed and feed across the nation. Farming as a tradition is so widely known and respected in Ireland, and has been around for so long that many farming skills have been passed down generation after generation for over two hundred years!

WHAT ARE SOME TRADITIONAL IRISH FOODS AND DISHES?

The potato is a well known major staple of Irish cuisine. Traditional dishes made with potatoes include Boxty, a potato pancake, and Shepherd's pie, a hearty dish made with minced beef or lamb, a mix of vegetables, and of course, mashed potatoes. In addition to their potato dishes the Irish have a varied diet consisting of many kinds of seafood and meat plus a wide variety of fruits, berries and vegetables. Soda bread is another Irish staple and is still made in many homes on a regular or even daily basis. Soda bread is hard and crusty on the outside, soft on the inside. It's called soda bread because the recipes call for baking soda as opposed to yeast.

WHAT IS IRISH COFFEE?

Irish coffee is coffee mixed with Irish whiskey and topped off with cream. Joe Sheridan, who was a chef in County Limerick in the 1940s, actually invented the beverage out of necessity! When a group of American passengers on a flying boat arrived to Ireland one miserable, cold and wet evening, Chef Sheridan served them a drink. He gave them coffee and added whiskey to it to help warm them up. When the soldiers asked what they were drinking the chef replied, "Irish coffee." And the name stuck!

WHAT IS THE HISTORY OF IRISH STORYTELLING?

Irish Storytelling is famous worldwide and it is a rich, cultural tradition of Ireland that has been passed down and evolved over many centuries. Many famous mythological creatures come from Ireland folktales such as banshees, faeries and leprechauns. Plus, many famous writers have hailed from the country as well! The tradition of storytelling in Ireland dates back to the Celtic bards. Bards were professional poets who were employed by rich patrons such as monarchs or noblemen and who told stories orally for a profession.

WHO ARE SOME FAMOUS IRISH STORYTELLERS?

Many famous authors have hailed from Ireland. Novelists such as Jonathan Swift, author of Gulliver's Travels, and Bram Stoker, author of Dracula both came from Ireland. Perhaps James Joyce is the most famous of Irish authors for his strikingly regional writings such as Dubliners and his most famous novel, Ulysses. Many of the stories from the ancient bards were originally passed down orally – they were told out loud and read – until later when poets started recording the bards' stories.

WHO WAS ST. PATRICK?

St. Patrick is named the Patron Saint of Ireland and is one of the most well known Catholic saints in the world. He was born in Scotland, not Ireland, in A.D. 387 and was captured at the age of fourteen during a slave raid and taken to Ireland. The story goes that during his captivity he prayed to God and once he returned to Scotland he dreamed that Ireland, the country, was calling to him, asking, "We beg you, holy youth, to come and walk among us once more."

Patrick then returned to Ireland and preached for forty years, traveling in poverty and converting pagans to Christianity.

WHAT IS ST. PATRICK'S DAY LIKE IN IRELAND?

In Ireland St. Patrick's Day is also called The Feast of St. Patrick. The holiday is a religious and cultural celebration observed on March 17th each year. The holiday is now celebrated in many other countries around the world other than just Ireland, including America, Great Britain, Russia and Japan. Today in Ireland the celebration of St. Patrick is primarily a cause for highlighting Irish innovation and creativity as well as a celebration of everything Irish – festivities will often include such activities as a parade, fireworks and even fun symposiums on how to talk Irish.

ARE THERE ANY OTHER FAMOUS HOLIDAYS THAT COME FROM IRELAND?

Believe it or not, Halloween also originated in Ireland! In fact, it was taken from an old Irish festival called Samhain. Samhain was originally a Celtic festival that celebrated and marked the beginning of winter. The shift in the holidays began in the 9th century with the Catholic reformation. All Saints Day on November 1st and All Souls Day on November 2nd were combined with Samhain to create a collective festival, what we now call Halloween. Children dress in costumes on Halloween in Ireland and collect candy, just as they do in other places around the world.

TELL ME ABOUT THE GAME CALLED "MR. FOX"

Children in Ireland, like anywhere in the world, play all different types of games. But one of the most popular traditional children's games in Ireland is called Mr. Fox. In this game one child is the fox while the other children stand apart facing each other with the fox in the middle. The children say, "What time is it, Mr. Fox?" The fox then replies, "One o'clock," and the children slowly step towards him.

This repeats until the fox decides to answer "Dinnertime!" at which point the children all turn and run from the fox, trying not to be tagged. The person who gets tagged becomes the next fox!

TELL ME A LITTLE BIT OF IRELAND'S INTERESTING HISTORY

Stone tools have been discovered in Ireland, in part leading archaeologists to believe that settlers arrived in Ireland as early as 3500 B.C. The famous Celts arrived much later, around 700 B.C. These diverse and technologically advance people would thrive in Ireland for nearly 2,000 years! When the Vikings arrived in the ninth century A.D. parts of modern Ireland were founded, including the capital city of Dublin. In 1948 most of Ireland gained its independence after many years under British rule.

WHAT LANGUAGES ARE SPOKEN IN IRELAND?

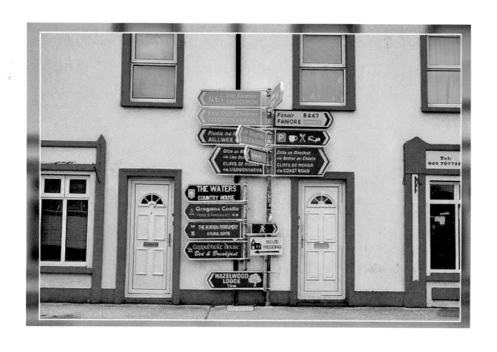

Ireland's official languages are Irish, or Gaelic, and English. Irish is primarily the second language for most residents, English being the first. English spoken in Ireland sounds much different than English spoken in Great Britain and America. The phrase, "What's the story," meaning, what's the news, is originally an Irish saying. There are also no words for yes or no in the Irish language. But you can still answer yes or no, you just have to do it a little differently. The yes or no answer to a question like this: Did you sell your house? would be either: sold or didn't sell.

TELL ME A LITTLE BIT ABOUT IRELAND'S ANIMALS

Interestingly enough, there are many types of animals found in Ireland, but one animal you won't find is a snake! This is because there are absolutely no wild snakes in Ireland! There are no turtles native to Ireland as well. Since Ireland is barricaded by sea, many mainland animals are prevented from crossing over. For this reason there are also only three kinds of amphibians and only one kind of lizard found in the wild in Ireland!

WHAT IS THE SIGNIFICANCE OF THE SHAMROCK?

The shamrock is a traditional and well known Irish symbol. The shamrock, which is a type of clover, is in fact the national symbol of the country and is represented alongside a harp. Tradition says that St. Patrick used the shamrock as a symbol of the Holy Trinity in Christianity, one petal each to represent God the Father, Jesus the Son and the Holy Ghost. The Irish also believe that the shamrock brings good luck, and they have influenced this belief around the globe.

TELL ME ABOUT IRISH FAERIE TRADITION

Irish Faerie tradition is rich and even tells us of the origins of fairies. Faerie, spelled with an e instead of an i means all things unnatural or mythic, including fairies, elves, trolls and other creatures like the banshee, which is an Irish fairy woman. The original Irish fairy tales were called the Tuatha Dé Danann and told how fairies came from the sky and other islands in the north of the world. Their ancestors became the Irish people. One of the most famous Irish writers of all time that shares traditional Irish tales taken from the Tuatha Dé Danann is Alan Garner.

WHAT IS ST. PATRICK'S CATHEDRAL?

St. Patrick's Cathedral is one of the most famous churches in the world! History and stories tell us that the Cathedral was where St. Patrick, the patron saint of Ireland, would baptize his Catholic followers. The cathedral was built in 1220 and is still used as a functioning church today. Tourists from all over the world come to visit St. Patrick's Cathedral, which is also known for its beautiful architecture and ornate decor.

THE PLACE WITH THE LONGEST NAME IN THE WORLD IS IN IRELAND

Out of all the different places in all the world, one special location in Ireland is known for its extremely long name. There is an expanse of land between two waters in Ireland called Muckanaghederdauhaulia.

The twenty-two-letter word means 'ridge' and is representative of the actual 470-acre townland in the ridged area between the waters.

WHERE IS SCOTLAND?

Scotland is located in the northern part of the United Kingdom, which includes Scotland, England, Wales and the northernmost portion of Ireland. Scotland covers about one third of the United Kingdom's total landmass. Located off the western coast of continental Europe in the Atlantic Ocean, Scotland is still a European Country. Scotland actually has two names; the Gaelic name for Scotland is Alba.

WHAT IS THE CAPITAL OF SCOTLAND?

The city of Edinburgh is the capital of Scotland but you'll be surprised to learn that it is not also the biggest city. Glasgow is bigger than Edinburgh in terms of population. Scotland only has six officially recognized cities. These are Dundee, Glasgow, Inverness, Stirling, Aberdeen and of course, Edinburgh. Edinburgh has been the capital of Scotland since at least the 15th century. The most popular and well-known site in Edinburgh is the Edinburgh Castle.

TELL ME A LITTLE BIT ABOUT THE PEOPLE OF SCOTLAND

Many people think of red hair when they think of Scotland, and rightly so considering Scotland has a higher percentage – eleven percent – of red haired residents than anywhere else in the world! However, this is a far cry from everyone having red hair as the stereotypes suggest. In fact, you may be surprised to learn that the Scottish people have a heritage that originated in many other parts of the world! The native people to Scotland were actually called Picts, which translates to painted people, because of the ways in which they used to paint their bodies.

HOW MANY ISLANDS DOES SCOTLAND HAVE AND WHAT ARE THEY LIKE?

Scotland has nearly eight hundred total islands but man only populates 130 of them. The islands each have their own unique attributes and offer diverse wildlife and rich, lush landscapes. Rugged mountains found on the islands of Orkney or Shetland, and bird sanctuaries like the one found on the Isle of May, are just a few examples of the amazing natural discoveries to be made while exploring the Scottish islands.

WHAT IS THE EDINBURGH CASTLE?

The Edinburgh Castle is a massive fortress that dominates the breathtaking skyline of Scotland's capital city. The rock on which the castle is built has been occupied since as early as the Iron Age! That means people have been living on that mountain for over three thousand years! Edinburgh Castle was built right into the rock on the giant mountain, but we are not exactly sure when the site was built. Today the castle is both a tourist attraction and a historical conservation site.

TELL ME ABOUT OTHER SCOTTISH CASTLES

Scotland is definitely known for its many castles; in fact, did you know there are over three thousand castles in this small country? Some of these castles are actually some of the oldest known castles in Europe! Because the country spent so many years at war there was a need for strongholds and buildings to protect the people – therefore, many fortresses, or castles, were built over hundreds of years. Some are built high up on hills, like Edinburgh, while others are built with the ocean waves pounding in around it. People come from all over the world each year just to visit some of Scotland's castles.

WHAT TYPES OF FOOD DO THE SCOTTISH TYPICALLY EAT?

The Scottish people have a varied diet but are known for quite a few unique dishes. One of their most popular dishes is fish and chips, which is fried white fish, like Haddock, served with french fries or chips. Shortbread is another dish the Scots are famous for. Shortbread is a buttery biscuit or cookie and can be found in different varieties all across the country. Sometimes shortbread comes dipped in chocolate or with a jellied fruit filling. A famous Scottish drink is the Irn-Bru, which is a carbonated fruit drink, like a fruit flavored soda.

WHAT IS A TRADITIONAL SCOTTISH MEAL?

A meal called Haggis is probably the most well known of all traditional Scottish meals. Haggis is also the country's national dish! Haggis is made from a sheep – but not the sheep's meat! Rather it is made up of what is called the sheep's pluck, which means the sheep's heart, lungs and liver. These juicy bits are cooked with minced onion, oatmeal, suet, spices and salt and then mixed into a soup stock. Traditionally cooks would simmer the stew in the stomach of the sheep although now it is often cooked in big pots. Would you try it?

TELL ME ABOUT THE LOCH NESS MONSTER

The word loch means lake, and Loch Ness Monster is simply put, a lake monster. In the stories the Loch Ness lives in the lakes of the Scottish Highlands. Some people believe that the idea of the Loch Ness came from an actual animal that descended from the plesiosaur, an ancient dinosaur. However, despite this theory, modern scientists don't believe that the Loch Ness is real and they call it a modern-day myth. The stories of the Loch Ness Monster are so popular that some people have nicknamed the monster Nessie.

DID THE UNICORN COME FROM SCOTLAND?

The unicorn, a mythical creature to some and a real creature to others, is actually Scotland's official National Animal! Unicorns are meant to represent beauty, youth, innocence and pride and are thought to bring joy and have healing powers. Unicorns are found in fiction stories all over the world but many Scottish people believe they existed at one point and are now extinct. What do you believe?

WHO ARE SOME FAMOUS PEOPLE FROM SCOTLAND?

There are a few world known authors that hailed from Scotland including Sir Walter Scott and Robert Louis Stevenson, author of A Child's Garden of Verses. The famous inventor, Alexander Graham Bell, who invented the telephone, also came from Scotland. Musicians Rod Stewart, Annie Lennox and Jimmy Shand are Scotland natives too, as are actors Sean Connery and Robbie Coltrane!

WHAT ARE BAGPIPES?

Bagpipes are a popular, Scottish musical instrument. The instrument consists of reed pipes that are attached to a bag. The player holds the bag in his arms and squeezes it while blowing into a mouthpiece, and in this way, music comes out of the reed pipes. The instrument is quite loud but fun to hear played. It is an old Scottish instrument and often played during ceremonies, like weddings, or during traditional festivals, or ceilidhs. The instrument is associated with Scotland but it's also played in France and Ireland.

WHAT IS A CEILIDH?

The people of Scotland often talk about a ceilidh, especially if you visit the Scottish Highlands. But what exactly is a ceilidh? A ceilidh is a traditional Gaelic social gathering like a festival or party, usually held in a town's hall or hotel. During the gathering traditional folk music is played while participants dance. Ceilidhs used to also be a time for telling stories and acting out tales for entertainment and songs were often sung. Today people still have ceilidhs and they are a fun way to do something traditionally Scottish.

WHAT IS HIGHLAND CULTURE?

Highland Culture is sometimes called Gaelic Culture and refers to the rich culture of the Scottish people from the Highlands. The Highlands' landscape was so rugged that the people who lived there were originally divided into clans and each clan was ruled by a chief. In fact, the kilt was developed during this clan time because they needed clothing that allowed them to climb over the rugged hills comfortably. The

Highlanders were said to be always ready for battle so traditions of strength came from their lifestyle. Some of these games include the hammer toss and the caber toss, which is a long, heavy pole.

WHAT LANGUAGES ARE SPOKEN IN SCOTLAND?

The Scottish people primarily speak English although Scottish English does not sound anything like British or American English. The native Scottish language, Gaelic Scottish, is only spoken by 1.5% of the entire population! The Scottish English is so different from English spoken elsewhere that sometimes foreigners have a hard time understanding it. For example, if you wanted to say, "You better just go easy," or "don't overdo it," in Scottish English you would say, "You'd better just caw canny."

WHAT IS THE SCOTTISH LANDSCAPE LIKE?

Scotland is made up of three major regions: the upper lowlands, the central lowlands, and the highlands and islands. The upper lowlands are just north of the United Kingdom and Scotland border, and most of the area is agricultural with rolling green hills and lush vegetation. The central lowlands are the most urban, populated and industrial of the three regions. Two major cities, Glasgow and Edinburgh, are located in the central lowlands. The highlands and islands are the largest of the three regions covering about fifty percent of Scotland's landmass. Dramatic and breathtaking scenery like deep lochs (or lakes), windy islands, and towering mountain peaks make up the area.

WHAT IS THE WEATHER
LIKE IN SCOTLAND?

Because so much water surrounds Scotland, since it is in the Atlantic Ocean, the weather will often change quite drastically, making it hard to predict. And, with so many different regions, the weather is different across the country. But one type of weather that you can depend on in Scotland is rain! Out of 365 days in the year, it will rain about 250 of them somewhere in

Scotland! Otherwise the climate is temperate and the country experiences all four seasons.

WHAT ARE SOME FAMOUS SCOTTISH MYTHOLOGIES?

Scotland is filled with rich stories and strong mythologies that have been passed down for ages. Some famous Scottish myths include the Loch Ness Monster, the Gift of Second Sight, and the Stone of Destiny. The Stone of Destiny is also called the Stone of Scone and it is a long block of redstone that was used to coronate the kings and queens of Scotland. The Gift of Second Sight is the belief that someone can see into the future! The Scottish myths also tell rich tales of fairies, goblins, sprites, and elves.

WHAT KINDS OF ANIMALS ARE FOUND IN SCOTLAND?

Because Scotland's landscape is so varied, so is its wildlife. The Scottish Highlands are known for having the highland cattle and red deer, which are both native to Scotland. You'll also find the golden eagle, red kite, red squirrel and wildcat in Scotland. Ocean animals include whales, dolphins, seals and even puffins!

WHAT ARE KILTS?

Kilts actually look just like skirts that are typically worn by women, but in Scotland, men typically wear the kilts. The kilts are knee-length and pleated, made of tartan cloth, which is a fabric with criss-crossing colors and lines, looking very close to plaid. Originally tartan was made by weaving bits of wool together, although now it is made from a variety of materials. The kilt used to be worn every day by the

Highlanders though now it is just used for special purposes, like ceremonies and festivals.